INTO THE HUSH

OF   THE

QUIET WINDS

DEDICATED TO MY ONE & ONLY

MOTHER :

JASMINE REGGIORI

FATHER:

(JOHN ANTHONY) YUNUS REGGIORI

ELDEST BROTHER

MOGAMAT YUNUS REGGIORI JR.

I had lost all three of them to cancer,

So i would like to donate some of the proceeds

To the Cancer Foundation of South Africa

And also to the (Gift of the Givers)

Two of the organizations, I hold so

close to my heart

and if you feel to donate directly

Please google them.

Your support would be much appreciated

Our bibles speaks of the able

being the distributors of God's wealth.

Help from all of you would go a long

way in helping me reach my dream,

of becoming a philanthropist

What would you do, if you knew

Your heart spoke a forgotten tongue

In soft whispering murmurs

That plays you like a violin song

I left it there in days gone bye

In the blushes of a sediment smile

But no more

Find my words, laid out

In the pages of my written heart

Walk in this here mile

On a bridge between the roses

And find my rain falling

From ink borne skies

Straight into your tepid heart

Contents

In your timeous deed   11

To dwell this airy loom   12

I know you feel my heart   13

Is it a fate fit for lovers   14

I've surpassed my love   15

How much I swoon   16

How beautiful she paints   17

Your beauty has all but taken me   19

I found myself today   20

A Mockingbird I could never be   21

Tonight , at dawn in the Vistas   22

I wove through the splinters   23

I watched the world swam by   24

There I was following moon trails   25

I was a jealous lover of those   26

Have you ever really

heard the whispers   27

In the darkness I found   28

I found in you, my love   29

These absent screams   30

Today my beautiful love   32

A few miles to the petulant seas   33

Oh! Beautiful soul   35

Dear lover, I know you are there   36

I could watch the rain   37

Where are you dear lover   39

My mind play these little games   40

At last my cage became undone   42

Shall we meet   43

Three yellow tailed sparrows   44

Oh! My full moon   45

Sitting high upon moonbeams   46

The halos of the candlelight   47

On dark sombre nights   48

Would we ever use the time   49

On the nights I've heard her whisper		50

She was one beautiful soul		51

I've been in the waiting		52

My heart fluttered		53

Your echos found me rising		54

By Tantric verse of Moon whispers		55

I found in you my love		56

The candle flamed a soft scented light		58

Under candlelit nights		60

When shall my tainted heartache ebb		61

Matters it now		62

Be then you the change		63

Be as always my yearnings		64

Still awake in the blissful silence		65

And shall we rise from the ruins		66

I felt a soothing kind of lullaby		68

Softly into the dark night		69

Fall now softly		70

I've seen the nosiness		71

Of a nibbling moon

In the dunes of days ... 72

Walk with me ... 73

Wayfarer ... 74

Avid souls reaping ... 75

I ran for the hills, not in retreat ... 76

Slurp at the taverns ... 78

I watch you silently exhale ... 79

Shyness permeates ... 80

Impressionable smiles ... 80

Stormy weathers ... 80

The wisps of dreams ... 80

Surf moon rivers ... 81

Slip a message ... 81

Like a sultry moon ... 81

Behind my eyes ... 82

Do ever I love poetry ... 84

I've walked your paths ... 86

I saw you dance ... 88

Upon the threshold ... 89

Lies can be truth 92

When shall my heartache ebb 93

Care you not that I live 95

I'm like a schoolboy blushing 96

Once upon a crime 97

How soft the air 98

The strewn petals of Sakura, felling 99

The days dial slow 100

This I've always done 101

She knows me well 102

In this moment of time 103

Love is a race of heartbeats 104

I'm infatuated 105

It is cosy warm 106

I have not known a soul whisperer 107

Into the path of wood's belly 108

Tonight remembered I those Bistros 109

I watch silently still 110

How wild the dawn 1 11

In your timeous deed

Of grooming

I've watched you

From across the stills

I fear I'm blushing

Flustered in the calm

Of your every heart beat

Every whisper of your soul

I'm the husband

To your Heaven

The marry of your dues

And at the final hour

I will wait for you

To say I do

MOGAMAT SHAFIEK REGGIORI

To dwell this airy loom

In a landscape

Of drifting meadows

And siphon the winds

Between whispers and a breeze

I find your floating ardor

Reaching out to me

Laid bare before my wings

And my need arose

To bridge the seasons

From my wintry bleak

To where you lay amidst the Aspens

I know you feel my heart

Beating in the Embers

Of your flames

It's how our dreams roam

Tethered, by the strings of our souls

Inscribed upon emparchment

Of ancient scrolls

Chiselled on the surface

Of Ophiolite stone

We mulled the gift of life

Together holding hands

As we pledged our Elysian hearts

Before we leaped

Into the mere whispers

Of the Cycle of Life

MOGAMAT SHAFIEK REGGIORI

Is it a fate fit for lovers

That we dwell intrinsic on moon cycles

The night is ours to dream

Entranced am I in you

From the days before

We chose upon Eden's bliss

Close your eyes and see

Our spirits are incomplete

For we bartered halves

Of each others plural hearts

I've surpassed my love

The days of my yearning

Instead I swim

The depth of my beautiful mind

Oh! how you made me smile

As we lay in the drawn out blushes

Of an afternoon July sun

And perhaps I ought to burst

The seams of those veritable dreams

And have the lush of those petals

Frame my ardor

Oh! How I love to reminisce

In the memories of you

MOGAMAT SHAFIEK REGGIORI

How much I swoon

Treading each timid frail

Above the stems

Where you the face of every flower

Blooms of nectar

You've let me drink once before

From your Orchards

Sweet sweet minted soul

I've inhaled your every ardor

Like fresh breaths of Sienna

From Autumn's promising glow

In all shades of you

How beautiful she paints

Landscapes that bath beneath our reach

And as dusk falls

It bleeds red the yawning skies

My mind begins to dwindle

Into the soft night of hearts borne to love

Shall I blow my breath of zeal

That reeks of my yearning through airy looms

Or shall I gently bow and hope

That my reflections, off the ponds

To the skies to the oceans

Carries my ardor, bouncing merrily

Into the pupils of her Sapphire eyes

If the world would still, I would

Draw a line and jump dominions

But I smile, for life's narrow paths

Plays but a tainted part

But time will collide our hearts to the blushes

And the soft falling of the rain

And in this life of Champagne skies

MOGAMAT SHAFIEK REGGIORI

We would spread our wings

To glide into our destiny

Syphon the gentle breeze

Over all worldly whims

And quench the longing of each others hearts

Your beauty has all but taken me

My mind fresh on sultry

And for hours I would stare into

My Alabasta dreams

You've found me in calm demure

Sweet woman

Amongst the Petunia

In a bed of dreams

Listening as the blossoms sing

Perhaps you'd lead my beating heart

Straight toward our future kin

Across the deafening stills

I found myself today

In the diversity of the blossoms

In the correlation of their hues

Amidst the blushes of all shades

Of you and me

And perhaps we ought

To heed their plight

Petunias makes a fragrant stance

Under the promise of the grimacing sun

To live interwoven in their cotton seas

A mocking bird I could never be

For I have not the voice my love

But a fledgling of words

Under the vastness of the blue skies

No matter how you crave, I may be

But I'm a Pisces

To swim the deepest ocean

To your perpetual heart

So I would dive beyond the reaches

Where corals glow, to find you

The most precious pearl

In the chest of the deep blue seas

Tonight at dawn, in the Vistas

I'll comb the strands of eternity

In the ousting of the clouds

The cumulus prepares the tears

Of weeping angels

To fall, to feed, to heal

And I, aloof of the whispers

Reminisce subtly

In the aromatic scents

Of elusive hearts

I wove through the splinters

Of my dying day

Where warriors lay slaughtered

In vain display

With a sword that vouch for mayhem

Sworn against the chaos reign

Wielding hope that served us blood

Upon the coffers

No mercy for this day

To face me is to tremble

Upon your stickly bones, nay!

MOGAMAT SHAFIEK REGGIORI

I watched the world swam by

In the rafters of the whitewashed seas

And I focused on the twinkle drops

That too dripped from flailing

Lavish trees

I slowed down

To heed the voice of silence

That Mother nature weaves

She knew me well

The mother of my being

She gave me Tropical Savannas

Wherein I could dwell intrinsically

& lazily lay about the reeds

There I was following moon trails

Amongst the ides of May

That changed my mood

To howl the scold

Into the middle distance

Ahoooo!.....

Black night of terror

That scatters worldly grim

And by the darkness

Of a Crimson moon , starkly stained

Against a midnight sky

I own the night with my reticent eyes

MOGAMAT SHAFIEK REGGIORI

I was a jealous lover of those

Who yearned to infest

Upon her Elysian heart, to breathe

In the air of her tepid love

My lover, she was no Nun

And showed much promise

Of an ascetic ardor

Across the twilight

I craved to fly

To ebb the silence

Between our ocean's tides

But being a Pisces

I swam the starry night

To find new depths

In an undercurrent to her heart

Have you ever really heard

The whispers

From distant forest glades

It Flung, sailing the cordial breeze

And crashed against heart flesh

To upset the rhythms to your lungs

Fresh spurts of breath

upon gaping timbres, lures

The senses into inertia

And releases Endorphins

To opiate our woken whims

To live, to love, to cherish

And embrace nature's gift to pliant hearts

MOGAMAT SHAFIEK REGGIORI

In the darkness I found

Your brightest aura glows

Along the riverbanks

Lady of the lake

That squeezed light from

Her fractured heart

The Sakura petals twirled

In scattered beauty, still

To mend the rifts

& I bequeathed the moon

With your eternal bliss

To shine forever bright

I found in you, my love

That midnight's hour dreams

Of emparchments, to gather

The written heart

My whispering soulstress

Elixir of my being

Flutters arose

From within every beat

Of my little murmuring heart

Between the Aspens

In spring's willowy night

Or amongst the clouds driven

Our yearning remains untamed

Unsated lust

Ode to our tethered love

These absent screams

I hold inside me

An emptied voice

Squalls

Where only silent breaths

Remains be staged

For to spurn a rented whim

Where would my heart belong?

When you have gone

Before me

Dear minted one

Where the drudged waterfall flows

Down bleach stained walls

Naked wanes remains

Tethered to silence

Indented, in the haunting

Of my soul

These sediment bones

grows cold

Make my bed warm

For I want a coming home

To you

Whether it be only just

in candlelight dreams

But you could always sedate me

Embrace me yet my love

MOGAMAT SHAFIEK REGGIORI

Today, my beautiful love

Lets arise at dawn

& wait, as the sun's tantric rays

Travel past foreign skies

In search of interceding eyes

Risen from the embers

Amidst our dreams

Reality embarks upon life

Where the shadows of your smiles

Hung over me like a street lamp

In the comfort that you are real

& for my silent shudders

Watching those lost strands

Pervade your indigenous eyes

This could ultimately be

My forever unfurling of time

A few miles to the petulant seas

I heard you sing, vivaciously

Amidst the Aspens

Finding its sway between the leaves

As you sung for doting hearts

& I was all in, in adoration

Your canticle resonated

Into the night's sombre skies

Until the dawn squeezed

Through the crack of time

Be our hearts merged

Enraptured in each others touch

Your voice courted me

To float non-perturbed

Into your loving arms

Sing me a river

& I'd swim

Upon the surface of your soul

Dear lover

Embibe upon me, all that you are

For I'm perused by your very ardor

Oh! lover sing me that song

MOGAMAT SHAFIEK REGGIORI

On the Ivory of the old Clavier

Like Nina Simone

& you my heart will ensnare

Like cool droplets, dripping upon my soul

Melt me my lover

But pour me gently into the Riviera

Into her rushes

So I may wade nightly, from your seas

Oh! beautiful soul

How you've tamed me

As if English had a hidden

More seductive tone

In your written Odes

You have shackled me

Bleeding your love

To pump tediously

Through my raving heart

So march I, upon the Ides

In Eden's adolescents

& smile at its sworn term

Close the rifts of freedom

Serve me life to thee

MOGAMAT SHAFIEK REGGIORI

Dear lover, I know you are there

But always there, beyond my reach

Giving me a reason to love

For your mists, wraps itself

Around my being

To expel the immiscible

Decanting the whispers

Though I long to see your light

In the valley of darkest night

For only your proverbial hand

Can lift me

From the bottom

Of these earthen seas

Where I parade

Amongst the wilting reeds

I could watch the rain

Mercilessly falling

& water down the glass panes

In that all familiar way

How it puddles

Upon the sagging floors

Splashing about the feet

Of weary stragglers

Lost along the Bay

& I, feeling the cozy glow

Of bleeding flames

Searing upon my naked truth

If you weren't here today

Running dainty touches upon frail

What was I to do

But watch it speak in braille

Against the clarity of the window panes

These rains kept you nestled

Within my needy arms

MOGAMAT SHAFIEK REGGIORI

So keep on falling

& we would listen still

To the whispers

of your gentle song

Singing in the hush hush

Where are you, dear lover

Strewn wide upon the Ocean's rim

My mind is lost within its mist

Roaming through its salted stills

Thus be, I write to you my love

A brethren of the pen

Wherever this message find you

May you gently accept its paper heart

Sail then silently back to me

Through the vapors of the seas

Where the moon sips on distant horizons

Till the quiet hour, when the Sun burns its lips

Come then back to me, my love

back to my murmuring heart

MOGAMAT SHAFIEK REGGIORI

My mind plays these little games

In the allure of the mists

Some days you stand bright

Like the Sun's rays

Through the Bay window

Aglow with an Auburn mane

& some days the rays

Creeps in from behind you

Removing those Eiders

From the blush in your curves

Enough to pride your flowery blooms

& like fruits from exotic Savannas

It ripens yet under my fluttery gaze

But were you ever here

Or is my eyes laced by trickery

Of what the heart yearns for

On one bent knee, I wish you would rise

Like the Sun over the horizon of the seas

At last my cage came undone

From behind steel ribs

Where I was to perch

Like a Canary or a posing Peony

When I'd rather be walking the catwalk

Now, at last I'd be free

To roam upon the earthen treats

& if I could, I would fly

Beyond the rafters of the sea

Away from these stills

I would spread my wings

Into the fluff of the soft clouds

Just to cypher the winds

Of messages she may have left for me

& air the woes of imprisoned hearts

Shall we meet

In our between the roses

Our bed of our dues

Allured am I to your whispers

My hair rose upon my skin

By every glance you honor me

Dare I dream, of how your silent breath

Could nurture me, over my face

So I beg to the wind

To carry my kiss

Through the blue planet skies

Transport it to where you lay

In the vistas

Amidst the swaying Heather

Three yellow tailed sparrows

This beautiful Sunday morning

Sitting on the threshold of my soul

Singing of purple rain

I infringed upon their disdain

& they flew circles around me

As if I would readily swerve

But I held my nerve

They could not take my breath away

For my heart was pure

Thumping like a carnival drum

& in the distance I saw her

A smiling Lily

Alabasta like the moon

The breeze carried her Eu De Parfum

MOGAMAT SHAFIEK REGGIORI

Oh! my, full moon

How far I run to tilt your brim

Across the multitudes

Longitude & latitude

But chase will I, you

Until the end of my days

For in my dreams we played

As atmospheric companions

Dancing upon cloud gardens

I'm yours my full-faced moon

But I'm the Sun

We're not permitted to stay

So in the quiet hour, you'd see me blush

Like the dawn, when I stand before you

& come would I, again & again

Trying to kiss your shade

Sitting high upon moonbeams

So I may yet stare

In through the windows of your soul

And amongst the thickets

Of the sultry blooms

I would love to sip the smiles

From your tender lips

That my kisses hopes to find

So wear me gently huddled

Amongst the orchard vines

Dear sweet lover

Amidst the blossoming blushes

MOGAMAT SHAFIEK REGGIORI

The halos of the candle light

Has infringed upon our woven hearts

While its paper lanterns

Floats silently out into the viscous seas

I have found my restitute

Even after our moans had stilled

For I salivate on your dewdrops

Contented in your rain

No matter what birth

No matter what day & age

But for you I'd come back

To love you again & again

On dark sombre nights

Where would I be?

If not for the words of your written heart

That inscribes itself upon my being

Even my breath, is as soft

As white noise whispers

My yearning drowned in wishful dreams

Where your silk has woven a path for me

Beyond the wispy tendrils

That smells of Autumn blooms

Speak to me, my love

Of how the waves calls out from the sea

Rushing to kiss our feet

Upon the white-washed shores

Of a long forgotten beach

MOGAMAT SHAFIEK REGGIORI

Would we ever use the time

To reflect

When faces are mirrored

In glass ponds

After the ripples subsides to a still

& if you saw foul

Would your colors wade to a gray

Like a darkened night

Where the breeze whispers softly in shame

The trees, they see the end-game

Ruffling their leaves in disdain

And the lies you tell yourself

Would simmer in the rain

So face it with the umbrella of a minted heart

For God accepts that

You've learned by your mistakes

On the nights I've heard her whisper

I've seen her from across the stills

Her mind dangles my shores

Splashing in the sultry waves

Of my ardent seas

And like moonbeams

She shines over my Orchard vines

Oh! does she play with my paper heart

Which at this point, is as thin as a cotton seam

Her winds of mischief sways in my fields

I would'nt dream of it any other way

But to relive the pain when she leaves

She was one beautiful soul

That spills magenta

And sentience, from her written heart

Her mind shines aglow

From beneath her soft tones

Framed by strands of blonde flails

From a luscious mane

Gifted beyond the brims of her bosoms

Her words floats upon you

Through ink born skies

How we cry for her rain

Or even to be bathed by her clouded shade

I've been in the waiting

Since Yesters Year

In the footfalls of the abyss

Silently brooding

Over the windows to my lovers soul

She remains the soft air

In the mistrals of the tender winds

Gliding purposefully

Over the golden rivenes

Always floating above the cotton seas

The very linen, I lay beneath

Dreaming of that Summer

When you had me at Hello!

MOGAMAT SHAFIEK REGGIORI

My heart Fluttered

Through the days

Before my vacant still

Oh! how your fringe flailed

I found her at the foot of a floundering hill

Alabasta, like a full face moon

Her tone shone bright

And lit the darkness to my Err

Lost in the spark of her bejeweled eyes

Trapped in its lust she smiled

And I blushed

Your echos found me rising

Avid, at the edge of the moon river

Lost was I in the sentience of liquid dreams

53

Pour into me

Your faint little ripples

That purges me on your truth

And gold atoms in the dust bind of your being

Find me waving

A yearning ocean of twilight seas

That whispers in water tunes

My breath rising as mist

From beneath

By Tantric verse of Moon whispers

That burdens upon my beating heart

I ponder silently oft the yearning

That lingers from your smiles

Then be there that dangling

That hypnotic tufts of auburn strands

That flails, infringed upon your Satin toned face

Your beauty still remains etched

In that peculiar place behind my eyes

That is reserved for my happiness

Behind the Phosphenes

Distinctive in laconic love

I'd absorb your every fragrant aroma

Your every sated mirth

For every part of you is a poem

Writing itself to unfurl in an intrinsic verse

I found in you my love

Your emotions

So tightly wound against

The pages of your all written heart

Every night's slumber

Found me soaring

Through skies of wonderment

Like a Falcon in search of the crumbs you left behind

Lure me yet, dear lover

Into your chasms

Behind the curtains of sunrise

Breaking as velvety glows

Into the nest of your heart, preserved for love

Such be the way, your prose indents itself

upon my being, like rain from ink borne skies

your words fills me to capacity, dear soul

& every night my dreams takes the long way home

For only love poured

From those sweet cherry lips

& be I the man to affirm the breath of you

In soft whispers

The candle flamed a soft scented light

& there you lay, sprawled before my eyes

In the acumen of the quiet hour

I could sip for Eons

Off your slopes of curvaceousness

That could never quench my thirst for more

I thought you would be lost to me

When the flames ebbed it's fiery glow

Only to find,your light burned

Brighter than the sunrise

Oh! purest heart

Your whispers would remain forever inscribed

Upon the surface of my soul

For you've imbibed on this lover

Like the chorus of a never forgotten love song

You became that candle

Burning bright the flames of lust

My purest delirium

A dewdrop that dripped

Into the midst of my being

Wetting my appetite for love and but a kiss

From your ever inviting lips

& this time would you stay past sunrise

So we may feast upon the blossoms

In their lushes bloom

That too yearns to meet you

So you may smell the fragrance of their petals

For like them that blushes in the dawn

You too complete me dear soul

MOGAMAT SHAFIEK REGGIORI

Under candlelit nights

Of harvest moons

Better sweet I lay

Lost in the mist of a lover's trail

& wish for your soft breath

To flame my silent ardor

Lest we rise into twilight skies

That could intercede for our hearts

Our paths would remain frosted

From millions of miles apart

& though be I, a dreamer

My dearest love

I can only hope you dream of me too

When shall my tainted heartache ebb

My better dreams roams free

Dwindling the Oft passion of her blooming heart

I see her printed words

Floating over the soft clouds

Giving me pleasure

Like the cools of a silent breeze

Yet, in yearns

I longed for her voice

To replace those silent whispers

So as to feather a touch upon my being

Matters it now

That the gray came calling

Within a lark's shadow

Gingerly, on quarterly stroll

For our pastel dreams

Evaded the whispers

Of bleak pasts

In slumbers journey

Fade quietly into the night

In deserted echoes

That hovers in silence

Of stolen tones

Be then you the change

To taunt the darkness

And drive the glimmer that

Sparkles bright into a lesser night

Little pin prick eyes

Glaring from distance stars

That silence splays across the twilight

And sail into the night skies

For the dawn is sure to rise

Beautifully flamed abirth

Be as always my yearnings

Release as sighs

Journeying the sprawls of time

Dancing through the hues

Of crimson skies

Pierce it then the facades of the seasons

Like white noise whispers

Softly gentle, with a seeming blush

Where be my season in the Autumn glades

Dripping like honey upon my soul

In tendrils of a scuffing breeze

Wispy, through a yellow sea of fallen leaves

Still awake in the blissful silence

Of slumber's night

My inherent being crosses the ripples

In resilience of uttered dreams

Find my searching heart, dear lover

Right there beside you

Where my visions yet twirls

And my mind whispers

Through the rising mists of a thousand worlds

Quench thee then, my yearning

Not of haste, but slowly

Upon the shadow of your soul

And shall we rise from the ruins

On that fateful day

With what to say, but I have

Or I had and where thus is it now

Gone where the time has gone

With a one way ticket amidst the thickets

Of all our Yesterdays

Like dust it flew into the harrowing winds

Blown into faint ripples

Cascaded upon the baron earth

But Dawn's record has you torn

As an assailant upon humanity

In deeds, disgraced

And be your father mourns

And so too, for your kin

Is that no place for a king or queen

But who for you shall intercede

But the greed

And who's tears shall be sweetened

I felt a soothing kind of lullaby

That travels from deep inside

Your sweet kindred eyes

A silent lure

That sparks my fire

Burning flames deep within

The mantle of my core

Beautifully thwarted in misty chasms

Thus be any given day I'd sing

In the chorus of your soul

Chanting along, in the spine of the glades

Swimming those open sea of leaves

Amidst the Cypress trees

But bathed be I, in your company

MOGAMAT SHAFIEK REGGIORI

Softly, into the dark night

The moon's shadows

Dances on the curbs

Under the street lights

And whispers songs

In spilled toned voices

Heaving hearts, reach

Into pastel dreams of minted days

Throw a little color my way

And watch me stroll into

The good night

Orevuar !!

Fall now softly

Into my kind embrace

And hear my heartbeat whisper

Peruse my murmurs that lay fluttering

In my souls nether flames

Those sizzles by your lingered purr

And your softened gaze renders me inebriated

In the midst

Of an ecliptic beam

By moonstruck I'm enamored...

Deranged

MOGAMAT SHAFIEK REGGIORI

I've seen the nosiness

Of a quiet nibbling moon

That travels with serene in silent whispers

Across a vivid noon

Staring and flaunting

With heartless guilt

And contemptuous

Snares that shall not wilt

And when or why would I restrain

When I, myself ensnared on the

Enraptured strings of its invisible veins

In the dunes of days

Where the flowers' hue

Parts with intrinsic reigns

With petals strewn, amiss

As their scattered beauty stills

Like fallen fossils of wind and swirls

Weepy hills lay filled of sorrow

As they blew away of ageing decay

Into the path of death's gobble

Destiny lay in a sea of colour

Of life and death and the rising souls

That floats into the forever tomorrow

Memories ~ born of Yester

Lay silent in the abyss

Walk with me

Through the gardens

Of silent bliss

Where twinkling dewdrops drips

From the flailing seas

of orchard vines

And the whispers of ruffling leaves

Peruse our sanity with ease

And do we sway

And breath

Wayfarer

From across the stills

I trail the silent wake of slithers breeze

Where the moon glimmers

In search of your residue

Your shimmering beads of restitute

Like exuberant petals of your evening glow

Walk with me through halos

Of a time mirrored amidst the twines

Under the soft velvet of a dusk filled sky

Avid souls reaping the misty dawns

As the sun's flames breaches our skies

Our aching hearts blush

To be sun-kissed gently upon our cheeks

In the whispering breeze

We silently lay

As our passion roared, sizzled

I fear I've been imprisoned

In the haze that I tread with a withering frail

For you've read me, my stills

I ran for the hills, not in retreat

From my aches and sorrows

That stalks the open seas

That morning I felt my eye twitched

Now wait do I, praying

Eyeing the fortitude for a feathered breeze

To whisper the return of my evergreen

Hold my demons reigns

The salt in the water

Holds them away

And I shall rub salt

In the wounds of earth

To keep them at bay

My tears runs like rivers

In the Marshland streams

For as you finally came

My croaking timbre gaped

From my weaving heart

But my yearning floated

Quietly into the distant skies

Slurp at the taverns

Of my dripping ravines

And mask my scented need

That rues out sweetly

Over the dawn's rising flute

The sun too would sing

My mind drifts blissfully thwarted

Through the passion

Where lay I sprawled in misted gaze

My tyranist saint

You ardently bequeath me

I watch you silently exhale

Your tender breath

Over empty paper moons

And as magic, invisible poems

Appear and crusted itself

Upon the fore

Oh! How I love your purple rain

Slide me over the hills

In the rushing of the dawn

Feather me your worldly whims

And stand I beneath it, as it falls

Like floating Sakura that fell

Into my swoon and but I swooned

In all that I live through in this beautiful life

And in my dreams, follow me into

The middle distance & make me dream of you

Shyness permeates

& blossoms

On crimson cheeks

Impressionable smiles

Sculpts indentations

Into my captive heart

Stormy weathers

Keeps her nestled

In my needy arms

The wisps of dreams

Slips silently mourned

Into a rising dawn

Surf moon rivers

In haste

But measured flight

Slip a message

Beneath my cage's door

& the door in itself

Would be no more

Like a sultry moon

Of the twilight skies

Your reflection

Rowed in on a tidal wave

MOGAMAT SHAFIEK REGGIORI

Behind my pining eyes

Lives far distant remnants

Of ancient cries

Memories of yesterdays

Shining a dull weary lure

Over my life's toiled maze

Like misted glass

On frothy nights

Sandblasted

Hiding behind mirrors

Shine your reflections

Upon my gaze

For that's what remains

Of a once soulful knight

Armored glass windows to my soul

The witch's curse

was variably foretold

But of you I ask

To brake these shackles

With mere kindness in an act of love

Do ever I love poetry

Poets & Authors of the heart

That blends music with a fine piece of art

& toast its equivocation with wine

A culinary blend of two tale deliriums

Harken into existence, for in time

Its perilous dreams

Lures the senses into rhyme

They make the moon

Kiss the sun

And dip their feet into the ocean

To soak up its tranquility

Poetry is the Tundra, romantics

Of our souls journey

The blend of physical elation

Against whimsical ought

Stanzas and rhymes

That phrases a moment

Against a backdrop of time

Strutting along on the catwalk

MOGAMAT SHAFIEK REGGIORI

I've walked your paths

Dissecting the woods

And heard your whispers

Of a thousand forgotten tongues

The rivers bled its soul

Like a woman in Ghaid

And it cheers in Masquerade

And the leaves flutters

In the trees that drops its cones

And feeds it seed

To the young and old

Sing along my humming birds

Like the pied pipers of the woods

With your angelic tunes

That plays with flutes

Fly me my floating soul

Through the nurturing woods

That sprouts its blooms

With aromatic scents of you

I too will lose myself

In your wings forever tamed

I saw you dance

In the Dandelion fields

And sway with their gentile

As you absorbed a kiss

From the sun's nether glows

My tainted sight floated

Like fairer dreams

Into a misty flaunt

I've fallen

As if I've heard your swan song

Even though my wings be minted

To fly far beyond distant horizons

Into a seasonal charm

But my eyes and stolen soul

Remains hidden

Softly embraced in the crevice of your heart

Upon the threshold

Of my laden eyes

Where the hours looms

And the ferns sprawls

As high as the trees

Over our hidden paths

My soul is imprisoned

Behind paper bars

Where tufts

Of melancholy verses graze

There be your roaming eyes

That tears as blades

Into the printed bleed of my heart

Silent whispers shifts

As slithering echoes of flames

Against my dawns' record

And my puddle of shadows builds

Slowly still

Amongst the reeds, in gentle waves

Betroth be my gentle ardor

Rest the windows of your soul

Upon the rain of my ink borne skies

And find my tears of joy

Your brightness bleaches

The night sky

And your shadow cast light

Upon mountain sides

Fill thyself upon my echoes

With your whispering tongue

Straight from my weeping heart

And I'd dance with you

Under a midnight sky

So the moon could glance at us

I would remain alive, entranced in your eyes

MOGAMAT SHAFIEK REGGIORI

Lies can be truth

Truth could be lies

Death could be the end

With sad goodbyes

Or another beginning, adorn

Even a continuation

From before we were born

So do I smile

Am I in contempt

Do I find peace

From master's exempt

I'm not a puppet

Yet, I love[d] him still

And all from my own free will

When shall my heartache ebb

You've shoved me into the darkness

When the light calls me still

And wrestle I the nerves

In a field of disgust

And a basket full of pills

Sedate me then, be I

You hover like a dark cloud

Feasting, not wavering

I feel concluded, empty

As if my surface is my all

And eludes all that is the rest of me

Eyes closed I dreamed

Of grazing an open field

Hoping a whirlwind shall lift me

Far beyond your vile eyes

Tearing at the cloth

That capes my severed soul

I too need a feathered breeze

To cool my blanketed being

To this day and age let it be known

I am that peculiar man

MOGAMAT SHAFIEK REGGIORI

Wrapped in a blanket

Then again, wrapped in a soul

86

Care you not that I live

By your every heartbeat

For you held me

By every second

Perilous stare

As you bloomed in the mist

And now I'm a traveller

Peering through the windows

Of your glassed over dreams

For a chasm to pull me in

Do you think of me

When you write your dreams

While you whisper it

To your chosen stills

MOGAMAT SHAFIEK REGGIORI

I'm like a schoolboy blushing

The brightest grin

As I lock you deep, deep within

I admit I love these trails

Your scattered petals makes

Laying paths, as it brittle

Off your over enduring heart

Someday you would too roam

These clouded gardens

And may I be that rose that enchants you

Once upon a crime

I craved to walk

The other side of life

In the black velvet

Of forever night

One million fireflies

Took to the skies

To light my way

But all I wanted was to stay

In the calm silence of our beautiful ether

Until, indeed dear God

You saved my soul by wake

With a golden veil aglow

It glittered upon me

The rise of a resilient dawn

You saved me with the scent of a pale white rose

MOGAMAT SHAFIEK REGGIORI

How soft the air we breathe

In this vintage panoramas

All forms of clades

Of a clandestine trait

Gathers for the unfurling of a new born spring

Slow down time and see

Their flirting wings

So dainty still, yet

There's beauty within

That gold sprinkled limbs

My eyes snaps the stills

Like a camera, with no flash

But these reticent pearls

Has seen with crystal clear clarity

The strewn petals of Sakura, felling

Scattered like drops from pooling water

As the Kawasaki belted through

The laden paths, it sprayed about the path

Like a scene of fairy mist

As it twirled through

The soft morning sombre air

And the side parked trees

Heaved their branches like limbs

To grab a hold of its kin

But gently it floats

Prolonging the essence of its being

As if it performed for me

And I held the beauty of their disdain

One soul could find beauty

In another souls rain

The days dial prudently slow

In an avocation of these luxurious

Stoned mason gardens

Where the shadows

Of unflung branches heaves

In the breath of a sordid wind

Arousing its motion to pre-ambate its sway

And the crawlers gnaws

At my feet

With an aching need

So I may pat its leaves like a pet in need

My quiet grows and with it, my hunger

To lurch feverishly

Into any thoughts of you

Live ye there

Where I picture you

This I've always done

Through so many moons of life

Sending spreads of billet doux

And now in digital frames

There's no perfume to spray

Over paper trails

So I send bouquets

Of soliloquy and vintage names

Sent from colourful landscapes

Of cloud gardens

Like a canvas of Monet

Breathing in the vistas

MOGAMAT SHAFIEK REGGIORI

She knows me so well

Even on days I stole a glance

And when I drank

From her ink fountains

Between the margin

Of her lines

In tethered dreams

The sun always burns

A bright lipstick glow

Upon our outstretched horizons

And pouts by burgundy tones

She grants me Shifaa

By a mere rendition of her written heart

In this moment of time

As you wake

The sandman rains dust

From my weepy eyes

Why do our Ether trade

Sleep for wake

When all I want is to make

Beautiful memories

I live for the rushes

Ensconced in the sphere

Of your printed heart

But as you arise

I search for the whispers of dreaming

MOGAMAT SHAFIEK REGGIORI

Love is a race

Of secular heartbeats

In the way my ardor swoons

At the very sight of you

Changing dresses like

The blossoms in season

One stolen kiss on shivers lips

And I sink, quenched on affection

Thus be, a dawn may rise

From my blushing aura

Hold me

Kiss me yet again

I'm infatuated

With the idea of loving you

Smiling in the shadow

Of your yesterdays

Where you roared like a lioness

The passion of your laughter

Echoed into the distance

Of the velvety twilight skies

Perhaps, it's those blushing dimples

On what I perceive to be

The pale of a full faced moon

MOGAMAT SHAFIEK REGGIORI

It is cosy warm

Afore the flames of the fireplace

As the winter logs chokes the air

In wood-smoke

Bleeding a colorful flame

Laid bare upon the fur of rams

Your sprawled limbs shimmered

And lost was I in a lover's whims

Gentle be my feathered touch

Whilst our souls entwined

Upon our flesh that heaven entrusts

Be not of untamed marry

& be I reserved upon these muliebrous swells

Ensconced in the whispers

Of the air you breathe

Our tears and sweat merging with the streams

I have not known a soul whisperer

Whom able to calm me

And allowed me to echo its words

Into the impeding horizon

Until that moment arrived borne of love

When we met before the dawn

In the after hours of fading dreams

The moon was elated to shine its reflection

Upon our impinging hearts

If we then had wings

We would have hovered over the belly

Of the vast emerald seas

Green on love ~

MOGAMAT SHAFIEK REGGIORI

Into a path of the woods belly

I went strolling

Amongst the dainty deities

Where soft ferns blossomed

In a dandelion rhapsody

The earth lay strewn with brushes

In blushed tones

Where in the violets, found I

My purple haze

I imagine the world will turn slower

So I may prolong the inhalation

Of these sweet scents

That lingers in the mists

Of tepid love

Tonight remembered I those Bistros

In the back alleys

Where you often sat and dined

Watching the crowds scurry on bye

Beneath the glow of the lamp posts

Bon Appetite

Sweet gentle woman

With the smile to lure an angel

Find me there, in the inviting eyes

Of a stranger

Of every minted soul

Craving the aroma of you

Just one day I would surprise you, my love

When finally we shall fall into each others arms

MOGAMAT SHAFIEK REGGIORI

I watch silently still

From my lonely balcony

Into the lashes

Of a sun stretching dawn

And its the little things you say

In the amorous gestures

Of your frivolous wordplay

I cannot see you

But I find you lingering

In the face of every moon-flower

& be but I smiled

With the thought of you

Alive inside of me

Buried within my murmuring heart

How wild the dawn

For which it scorns

So primitive

Of the life it born

Not waiting on the brittle

Of the bones

But to ensconce

The life it holds

Into the ether grows

The calm

Planted from the seeds

From the micro atoms

That is you & me

Which is we

To feed the blossoms

Mother knows her way

Mother Nature always has us placed

No free spirited gentile

Shall ever go to waist

& be, a better part of me/we

Finds residents

In the body of the roses

Or perhaps our vociferous voice

Keeps whispering like the leaves

Fluttering in the Sycamore trees

& passive yet, the idea of sipping our fill

Silently floating in a pond or a river

Like the milky white lilies

Where the core contains both you & I

The Pistil and the Anther

Sharing the same embracing smile

With our toes in the soil beneath

When last have I seen the winter rains
That auspicious time that compares
To the authenticity
Of the beautiful night skies
When the sub- season provokes
Searching tongues to drink
Before the dessert sand, it swallows

Was it fun, that my mother knew my pain
And that the future tossed me bain
That she saw how my health toiled
Like the seas, when I swerved
when the sun kissed me at noon

She herself knew my route downstream
To the edge of the sea
Sickness beheld our Genes
Like a smile beholds my cheeks
For we were winterblossoms

And how we feared the Sun
That grasped at our heated brigades
I found this withering frail, but a blip
for the Ocean knew our names
And only time will tell
Of which derelict my way came
But she's a nurturing sea
with her white rafters
Like the frills of a dress
That dances for me

She would honor me, kin of her being
To have me float in her bosoms
And upon the belly of her deep
A gentle being & for a while
I too may know, what the afterlife
Would like generously feel
like floating weightless in the emerald seas.

BY : M.S. REGGIORI

Author & Poet

Share the words
that melts my heart
& I will kiss the day you came

Thankyou for your kind support
I hope I have enticed you to continue
Reading any future releases. I have
Hundreds of unreleased poems in the
Process of being captured. Please watch
This space for further antholigies.
All intellectual properties reserved.

Lightning Source UK Ltd.
Milton Keynes UK
UKHW041052240322
400553UK00001B/28